# BELLS AND POMEGRANATES

James M. S. Tait
1903 - 1980

# Bells
## and
# Pomegranates

*with*
## Additional Poems

by
# JAMES M. S. TAIT

**JOHN RITCHIE LTD**
CHRISTIAN PUBLICATIONS

40 Beansburn, Kilmarnock, Scotland

ISBN-13: 978 1 907731 76 1

Copyright © Mrs E.M.R. Tait

Published by John Ritchie Ltd. 2012
40 Beansburn, Kilmarnock, Scotland

**www.ritchiechristianmedia.co.uk**

Typeset by John Ritchie Ltd., Kilmarnock
Printed by Bell & Bain Ltd., Glasgow

# CONTENTS

# Foreword

"Bells and Pomegranates" was first published in 1946 and contained a selection of poems written by James M. S. Tait between 1926 and 1946. After his death in 1980 a large number of manuscript poems were found amongst his papers; some of these had appeared in various Christian magazines, but most had not been published.

James M. S. Tait was a Solicitor by profession and well-known throughout Shetland. From his youth he was a member of the church at Ebenezer Hall, Lerwick. He was a regular preacher, an esteemed elder and a recognised leader of the church.

Ebenezer Hall was officially opened as a centre for Christian witness on 1st July, 1885, and it is fitting in this centenary year that "Bells and Pomegranates" should be reprinted, in a much enlarged edition, including nearly all the previously unpublished poems.

It is believed, that like the previous edition, the present edition will give much pleasure and spiritual enrichment to the thoughtful reader.

*George S. Peterson*
*Church Secretary*
*Ebenezer Hall, Lerwick*

*11th May, 1985*

# Prefatory

*Thou mayest add thereto* — 1 Chron. 22. 14

THY House, O Lord, is richly wrought
    With costly ores and rare.
The wisest and the best have brought
    Their choicest treasures there.
Yet while I view, with kindling eyes,
    Those riches, old and new,
Thy gracious tones my soul surprise —
    "Thou mayest add thereto."

So be it Lord, as Thou has said.
    Most gladly would I bring
Each little thing that I have made
    Touching Thy glorious King.
If aught Thy holy eye shall deem
    As pure and fair and true,
Vast though this gathered store may seem,
    O add my mite thereto!

# PARABLES IN VERSE

# Bells and Pomegranates

*A golden bell and a pomegranate, a golden bell and a
pomegranate, upon the hem of the robe round about*
— Exod. 28. 34

WITH holy awe and reverent pace,
    The Priest approached the Holy Place;
Attired in garments that became
The Place where God had set His Name.
His ephod shone with gold and gems,
While softly from the wreathen hems
The mellow music rose and fell,
From 'a pomegranate and a bell,
    A pomegranate and a bell.'

To-day there's still a Holy Place,
An Altar, and a priestly race.
A godly order still obtains,
The "Pattern of the House" remains.
Shall I invade that sacred shrine
And jangle through its calm divine,
With clamorous notes that plainly tell,
'No pomegranates, but a bell —
    Another bell — and another bell'?

O for the grace that knows to suit
The outward sound to inward fruit;
That knows how well the music blends,
When lips confess and life commends;
That, though with boldness coming, brings
No reckless touch to holy things;
But hems the priestly garment well,
With 'a promegranate and a bell,
    A pomegranate and a bell.'

# Princely Gifts

*If the Prince give a gift unto any of his sons, the inheritance thereof shall be his sons'; it shall be their possession by inheritance. But if he shall give a gift to one of his servants, then it shall be his to the Year of Liberty; after, it shall return to the Prince; but his inheritance shall be his sons' for them.* — Ezekiel 46. 16-17

O HE is princely in His giving! He
, With servant-gifts and son-gifts loadeth thee.

His servant-gifts are good. His kindly care
Through all thy years of toil thou mayest share.
Raiment and food, and daily strength bestowed,
Shall make the labour light, and ease the load.

Yet all these lavish bounties Time doth bound.
For when the Trump of Liberty shall sound,
Thy servant-toil and servant-needs all o'er,
Thy servant-gifts, unmissed, shalt thou restore.

But, ah, His son-gifts! These are best of all,
Never to fade away or know recall.
Thou art a son, and, if a son, an heir
Destined His own inheritance to share,
Not only till the Year of Jubilee,
But evermore, throughout Eternity.

# Apostolic Lodgings

*Up into an upper room* — Acts 1. 13

*Paul dwelt . . . in his own hired house, and received all that came in unto him* — Acts 28. 30

TWO houses art thou given wherein to dwell;
   Happy art thou, if both thou usest well.
To one thou climbest high, with willing feet,
Above the world, thy risen Lord to meet.
The other to the busy street stands open free,
That sin-sick men may come to meet with thee.

The breath of Heaven thy "upper room" delights;
Thy "hired house" the groans of earth invites.
So with a dual grace thy life is crowned:
Communion pure, and sympathy profound;
Love to thy Lord, and love to all around.

# Weeping in Heaven

*I wept much.* — Rev. 5. 4

WHAT, tears in Heaven! Can it be,
   A saint in tears in that glad place?
Yes, I could weep, as well as he,
   If there I missed my Saviour's face.

'Weep not. Behold!' No matter where,
   Our tears are dried if He appear.
Without Him, we'd be mourning there;
   With Him, we can be joyful here.

7

# Jehovah Shammah

*In the way.*
*In breaking of bread.*
*In the midst.* — Luke 24. 35-36

I WALKED abroad, and on Life's toilsome way
   He met me there.
In home's sweet peace, my hearth at close of day
   He came to share.
I sought His own, of Him to hear and tell
   In converse rare;
When lo! a hush, a sudden glory, fell:
   The Lord was there!

# Entering the Cloud

*The thick darkness where God was.* — Exod. 20. 21

OFT in Life's sunny summer, O how near
   My God had seemed! His voice how sweetly clear!
In every fragrant bloom that flourished fair,
I saw dear token of His instant care.
Sudden the shadows fell. The sun withdrew.
Deeper, more dread, the darkness round me grew.
'Where now is God?' I cried. Mistimed despair:
Lo, where the cloud was thickest, God was there!

# The Fig Tree

*When He had looked round about upon all things . . . He*
*went out unto Bethany.* — Mark 11. 11

HE came, He looked on all. With eye of flame
   He scanned the shrine that bore His Father's Name;
Then, turning, left behind that fruitless tree:
What there He sought in vain, He found at Bethany.

He comes, He scanneth still; before His eye,
Naked and bare, all shams and falsehoods lie.
Searcher of hearts! O findest Thou in me
Mere foliage or fruit? Salem of Bethany?

# The Dignity of Service

*His blood-servants shall serve Him.* — Rev 22. 3

*And they shall reign for ever and ever.* — Rev 22. 5

BEFORE the Throne there's neither toil nor care;
No wearied limbs, no anxious minds, are there.
Yet though they rest indeed who see His face,
No one is idle in that happy place.
The saints above two diverse tasks combine —
(What man divorces, God can intertwine) —
They are His servants, and they serve amain,
Yet, e'en while serving Him, they also reign.

O teach me, Lord, that of this heavenly art
I may beforetime learn a little part!
For my proud heart would fain for honours pray,
Yet from the bond-slave's taskwork turn away.
O give me grace to stoop! For otherwise
I sink the lower as I seem to rise.
And let this truth my life's endeavours nerve —
None truly reigns but those who truly serve!

# Faith's Education

*A desert place.* — Matt. 14. 15

*A mountain apart . . . alone.* — Matt. 14. 23

*The sea, tossed with waves.* — Matt. 14. 24

THE desert place, the mountains lone, the troubled sea,
These are Thy schools, there I may learn of Thee.

The broken Bread, the Prayer on high, the outstretched Hand;
The hungry fed, the sinking saved, the ship at land;
The baskets filled, the waves subdued, the tempest past;
The plan, the power, the grace from first to last;
I con my lesson o'er, and still spell out —
'O thou of little faith, why dost thou doubt?'

9

# Doorkeeping

*Shut thy door* — Matt. 6. 6

*Open the door.* — Rev. 3. 20

M AKE me a wise Doorkeeper, lest
Ill things defile the closet of my breast.
Care of the World; its vain, deceitful pelf;
The praise of men; the love of pampered Self;
These come, and many more, with thronging feet,
And at my little portal press and beat.

"Begone," I cry; — but fail to bolt and bar;
Soon as I turn, the door is prised ajar,
And (faces changed and garb tricked out anew)
In sweep triumphant all the devilish crew.
What trouble now my sanctum to restore,
And all because I did not lock the door!

Make me a wise Doorkeeper, lest
I heed not Him who speaks, the waiting Guest.
Lest, busied much within with other things,
Him I leave out, with all the good He brings.
For shame! I'll draw the bolt, I'll turn the key;
This night I'll sup with Him, and He with me.
Life's dullest flagon brims with vintage o'er,
When Christ comes in at my heart's open door.

# The Place of Privilege

*Did I not see thee in the Garden with Him?* — John 18. 26

I T may be that the Lord hath favoured thee
More than the many; thou hast been apart
With Him alone in holy privacy,
And deeply learned the secrets of His heart.

If so, O watch and pray! For there is one
Who with malignant eye is watching thee.
If, favoured thus, thou still should'st be undone,
Satan indeed could boast a victory.

# The Net-Menders

Matt. 4. 21

J AMES and John were brethren: by the Sea
      They sat and searched their fishing nets to find
If there some broken strand or mesh might be,
      Which they with patient, skilful hand might bind.
They were experienced fishers, and they knew
That gaping rents let goodly fishes through.

So, while their partners fished, they in the boat
      Together sat, a-mending nets; and He
Who could the toil of busy Peter note,
      And called the bold apostle, 'Follow Me,'
Had also (Perfect Master!) work in view,
Suited for men like James and John to do.

Years have gone past — Still John, with watchful eye,
Observes lest things should fray with wear and strain;
Still seeks the mender's gentle art to ply,
      Still seeks to 'strengthen things that yet remain.'
With cords of Love he threads his needed, Truth;
He heals the schisms who mended nets in youth.

O Lord, I pray that in these latter days,
      When many strive, and rashly tear and rend,
Thou would'st raise up such men of tact and grace,
      The things that crumble and would part to mend.
Teach us, O Lord, and let us not forget,
Both how to fish for men, and mend the net!

# Beaten Gold

*They did beat the gold into thin plates, and cut it into wires, to work it in the blue, and in the purple, and in the scarlet, and in the fine linen, with cunning work.* — Exod. 39. 3

H E who the High Priest's garment scanned with care,
    Perchance might note, bright-glinting here and there,
      A tiny golden gleam.
That shining thread, wrought deep in fabrics rare
Of scarlet, blue and purple, by compare
      A trifling thing might seem.

But ah! if he the secret had but known —
What patient toil, what anxious skill were shown
      To spin that thread of gold —
With wondering admiration he would own
One such inwoven gleaming line alone
      A marvel to behold.

So have I sometimes turned me to admire
The holy vestments and the rich attire
      That noble spirits wear;
Yet have forgot the anvil and the fire,
Where they have hammered out the golden wire
      That shines half-hidden there.

# The Two Prayers

*Father, give me.* — Luke 15. 12

*Father . . . make me.* — Luke 15. 19

' G IVE me,' he prayed, the foolish, wiful boy.
    He thought that but to *have* was to enjoy.
A broken, sobered man, robbed, hungry, bare,
'Make me,' he prayed; and 'twas a wiser prayer.

Much wiser. My possessions may decay:
What I *become* can no one take away.
A man's true worth may be appraised the best
By what he was, not by what he possessed.

# The Scribe's Opportunity

Matt. 8. 19-20

*Said one to Jesus, all with zeal aglow,*
*'Lord, I will follow Thee where'er Thou go'*
*Strange, sad reply the wayworn Master made —*
*'The Son hath not a place to lay His head.'*

AH, scribe, how blind thou art! Dost thou not see
That *here* thou hast thine opportunity?
Man, fling thy door wide open! Bid Him come,
Feast at thy humble board and share thy home.
Bring thou the bason for those weary feet,
And gird thyself for lowly service meet.
Spread thou a couch for thine illustrious Guest;
Bring Him a pillow where His head may rest.
Thou fain would'st follow Him through all the earth:
Hast thou no room for Him at thine own hearth?

Alas, poor man! Things distant, brave and grand,
Shut out the humble duties close at hand.
With dreams of future greatness too engrossed,
He lets the priceless present hour be lost.

But dare I judge him? What in him I see
May have, perchance, its counterpart in me.
Have I the 'day of small things' rightly prized,
No task of homely charity despised?

For light and power have I not raised my prayers,
Yet closed my doors to angels unawares?

He who does not what little good he can,
Is no companion for the Son of Man.
Christ never bids them rise and follow far,
Who find no ways to serve Him where they are.

# The Secret of the Stairs

*He was taken up. —* Acts 1. 9

*They went up into the upper chamber. —* Acts 1. 13

THE Lord has gone on high; for we perceived Him
    Ascend in radiant cloud from Olivet;
But to that glory bright which has received Him
    We may not follow yet.

Our mortal feet may not ascend to Glory,
    Our mortal eyes see not the One we love;
Yet may we climb, and from earth's highest storey
    Commune with Him above.

Our upper room we'll make a nether Heaven
    With love's fair banner over us unfurled.
Though not to live in worlds above 'tis given,
    We'll live above the world.

# Giving and Taking

*The disciple whom Jesus loved saith . . . 'It is the Lord.' —*
John 21. 7

*Eli said, 'It is the Lord.' —* 1 Sam. 3. 18

NOT sceptic Chance, not pagan Destiny,
    Not Providence, impersonal and cold.
It is THE LORD! His living care for thee
Knows when to give, and when His gifts withhold.

Yea, when to take! Mayhap His hand hath reft
    That treasure dear thy heart could least afford.
Bless Him, that still to thee this grace is left,
    With chastened soul to say, 'It is the Lord.'

14

# The Place and the Person

*Judas also . . . knew the Place.* — John 18. 2

' T IS not enough that I should know the Place,
      Where Christ oft-times communeth with His own.
This nobler knowledge add, this greater grace —
To know Himself, and of Himself be known.

'Twere but a traitor's part to come all fraught
      With fervour feigned, presumptuously bold;
To hail Him 'Master' while I served Him not,
      To kiss His cheek when love was dead and cold.

# The Forgotten Sheaf

*When thou . . . hast forgotten a sheaf in the field, it shall
be for the stranger, for the fatherless, and for the widow;
that the Lord thy God may bless thee* — Deut. 24. 19

H APPY art thou, if from the toilsome field
      Thou reapest richly Wisdom's mellow yield.
A mind well stored, an understanding heart;
If these are thine, thou hast a princely part.

But as, perchance, from some high-laden wain,
Slips, unobserved, a sheaf of golden grain;
So here and there along the good man's path,
His ripe abundance leaves its aftermath.

A word of living truth; a thoughful phrase
Of counsel wise, of sympathy, of praise;
Forgotten sheaves, dropt half-unconsciously,
Like bread from heaven to starving souls may be.

Thrice happy thou, if such an one thou art;
For He who feeds Himself, the hungering heart,
Will *not* forget thy sheaves: will bless thee more
For those lost handfuls than thy garnered store.

# A Tale of Two Gardens

Prov. 24. 30-34    Song of Sol. 4. 12-16    Heb. 6. 7-8

C LOSE by the wayside, circled by a wall,
    I saw what seemed a garden rich and fair.
There daily fruit-begetting sunbeams fall,
    The dew by night distils unstinted there.
'Surely,' I thought, 'the orchards here will bloom,
    And pleasant fruits this favoured spot must yield;
The Master's barns be packed to offer room
    For all the produce of this fertile field.'

I nearer looked: I saw that noble wall
    Neglected lay in shameful disrepair.
Here bulged a sagging corner, soon to fall;
    A gaping breach lay unregarded there.
Boars of the wood and foxes from the hill,
    With noisome beasts and hateful creeping things
Passed in and out, tore up, and gorged their fill.
    Foul birds o'erhead outstretched their unclean wings.

Within the vineyard all was dire neglect;
    Untilled, untended: weeds grow tall and rank.
Thistles and thorns a prickly maze erect,
    The nettles flourish fast on every bank.
No fruit, no perfume, in the whole wide place,
    Nothing to please the eye or feast the soul.
O what a harvest when, in little space,
    The Master reaps, and fire consumes the whole!

It was the garden of the slothful man.
    The Master gave him this to dress and keep,
But he has spent, as fools and sluggards can,
    His precious days in indolence and sleep.
'A little more of ease,' has been his cry,
    'I have no love for toil and sweat and care.'
Fast comes his doom — a bankrupt knave to die,
    In want, in shame, in darkness, in despair.

There was another garden by the way.
From far I sensed the perfume of its flowers.
Spikenard and frankincense are there, they say,
Aloes and myrrh in all its spicy bowers.
Fountains throw up their living sparkling streams;
Deep limpid wells, sealed up from vulgar eye,
Are kept to cheer the Master's heart. It seems
That tree and shrub and herb in beauty vie.

Some blooms are there that blossom best, they say,
When from the balmy South the breezes blow.
Some fruits are ripest in the wintry day,
When stinging from the North come hail and snow.
But whether winds may blow from South or North
Fragrance flows out: the garden yields its all
To Him who bought it, cast its brambles forth,
And built its tower, and reared its girdling wall.

I craved the secret of this lovely plot:
'Sunshine and shower the same, alike the soil,
What hath this garden that the first had not?'
'Care unrelaxed, and unremitting toil!'
O be thou watchful every day, nor spare
The keen incisive hook, the probing hoe,
If thou would'st bloom with clustered blossoms fair,
If thou would'st fruit of mellow ripeness grow.'

# Earthly and Heavenly

*Consider the lilies of the field.* — Matt. 6. 28

*Behold the fowls of the air.* — Matt. 6. 26

HERE, where His hand hath lowly planted me,
My days are spent.
Nor ask I more: assured that where His will
Hath fixed my lot, His grace will nourish still,
I am content.

Yet, like yon bird that carols high o'erhead,
My spirit's free.
Far, far above the toilsome troubled scene,
I soar and sing, with not a cloud between
My God and me.

# "Whom the Lord Loveth"

Num. 4.

SAID a discontented Levite to his brother by the way,
'What a heavy, awkward burden Aaron's given us today!
With the scorching sun above me, and the path so rough below,
My soul is quite discouraged at the way we have to go.
Why should we Levites only be compelled such loads to bear,
While all the rest around us walk along without a care?
What are we worse than others that such evils we endure?
'Tis a hard, unequal world we exist in, to be sure!'

Then his fellow-bearer answered in a sympathetic tone,
'Yes, I know the load is heavy, and the way is rough, I own.
But do not be impatient, I beseech you, brother dear,
Nor envy those whose different lot much easier may appear.
Did God not choose us out to fill the place of first-born ones,
And shall we murmur if He now deals with us as with sons?
So far from vain repining, I should rather say 'Rejoice,'
Since the very weight you carry manifests Jehovah's choice.
Think not that God is cruel to you while kindly to the rest:
He often lays the heaviest load on those He loves the best.

Then mark with what considerate grace has everything been planned!
He knew the burden was too much for one alone to stand;
He hung it therefore on a staff that each an end might bear,
And thus in loving fellowship the other's burden share.'

'But then,' replied the younger man, 'Why all this mystery?
I would not mind so much, perhaps, if only I could see
The why and wherefore of it all, and what is hid within
This ugly outer covering of coarse, dark badger-skin.'

The other gently answered, 'No, 'tis not for us to pry
Into God's mysterious providence with unanointed eye.
Our part is just to shoulder what His wisdom may assign;
Faith neither questions nor resists nor doubts the will Divine.
God often wraps His purpose round that none can comprehend
What the meaning of the burden is until the journey's end;
But when the staves are then laid down, and dark veils all unfold
The heaviest load has sometimes proved a mass of shining gold.

Then let's not weary doing well, nor think our portion hard,
But rather have our eye upon the recompense reward,
Content meantime that we should have the evil with the good —
The same decree which fixed our load fixed, too, the Levites' food;
He who appoints the task provides the strength on which to draw —
Not as when Pharoh asked for bricks and yet withheld the straw.

Toil on, then, pilgrim Levite, nor despise the honour given,
To bear through dusty paths on earth the priceless gold of Heaven.
Faith not, you wayworn child of God, but as you feel the weight,
Remember the eternal joy, far more exceeding great.'

# The Lodger

*Lodge here this night.* — Numbers 22. 8

AH, thou that that dalliest with temptation and would'st fain
A little while thy fell guest entertain;
Think'st thou with morning light he'll clean depart,
And ne'er again come knocking at thy heart?

Vain thought! If once thy threshold he has passed,
That first success shall hardly be his last.
With bolder face, and with augmented train,
Another day shall see him back again.
Tenfold more easy then the downward way:
Tenfold more difficult to say him nay.

This truth, writ plain for every eye to see,
Is blazoned o'er the page of history:
The man who stood not firm while yet he could,
Shall find no strength to turn him when he would;
No, not though e'en an angel out of Heaven his way withstood.

# Love's Circuit

*We love, because He first loved us.* — 1 John 4. 19

*The Father Himself loveth you, because ye have loved Me.*
— John 16. 27

GOD loves me; and, as on His love I dwell,
My heart grows warm, and I can love as well.

I love the Son; and, loving Him, I find
I share a Father's love, strong, wise and kind.

O blessed circle! End there cannot be.
I still must love, and still He loveth me:
Loving and loved, throughout Eternity!

# Winter

*It was winter.* — John 10. 22

THE Everlasting Father is His Name.
His years fail not. No shade of change can fall
To dim His stainless lustre; for when all
Decays and ages, Christ remains the same.

Yet hath He known Time's changing seasons, too.
The vernal freshness; summer's glory brief;
The fruitful autumn and the garnered sheaf;
Chill winter's icy flake — all these He knew.

So when with numb despair I turn away
From some fair blossom withering Time has slain,
I find in Heaven a Heart that knows my pain;
A Heart that understands a winter's day.

He best can sympathise; He knoweth best
The texture of our being, woof and warp.
Yea, all the ten-toned strings of Life's great harp.
True Son of David, echo in Thy breast.

# The Undrawn Sword

*'Behold, here are two swords.' He said unto them, 'It is*
*enough.' — Luke 22. 38*

H ONOUR to him, true servant of the Master,
     Who bore the sword, and yet from strife refrained;
E'en as his Lord, through all that dark disaster,
     His hosts restrained.

The sword undrawn may tell of nobler merit
     Than his who wars to win the laurel-crown.
'Better,' 'tis writ, 'to rule aright the spirit
     Than take a town.'

Thy strength thy weakness is, if thou abuse it,
     Thy courage cowardice, if uncontrolled.
To have the power to smite, and not to use it,
     Is strength twofold.

*Only one of the swords (Peter's) was used. The other remained undrawn.

# Divided and Multiplied

*How many loaves have ye? — Mark 6. 38*

*When He had taken the five loaves . . . He brake the*
*loaves. — Mark 6. 41*
(Compare Mark 14. 22)

*They that did eat of the loaves were about five thousand*
*men. — Mark 6. 44*

Y EA, did'st thou place thine all into His hand,
     And did He mar it? O then understand
'Tis thus He deals with every loaf He takes;
Ever, before He multiplies, He breaks.

Himself was broken; for the famished soul
Ne'er could partake of Him, were He yet whole.
Alike in Nature and in Grace 'tis shown,
The corn of wheat must die, or bide alone.

See, then, this thing is true in Him and thee;
E'en as the Master, must the servant be.
In broken fragments must the bread be passed —
Made small at first, but multiplied at last.

# The Burden and the Song

*The service of the burden.* — Numbers 4. 47

*The service of song.* 1 Chron. 6. 31

ALL through the desert's sultry day
A weary load to carry;
Who envied then the toilsome way
Of Kohath and Merari?

Now priest and Ark alike find rest
Where God His temple raises;
And they who served with burdens pressed,
Now only serve with praises.

How perfect are the ways of God!
How just His compensation!
How long the path they humbly trod;
How high their exaltation!

No needless load on thee He'll lay,
No unrequited sorrow.
The burden-bearer of today,
Is the singer of tomorrow.

# The Masterpiece

*I will make him a pillar in the temple of my God, and he shall go no more out.* — Rev. 3. 12

SEE, the Sculptor's toil is ended,
Hammer, chisel, laid aside;
But the form his skill intended,
All the grace and beauty blended,
Every line symmetric, splendid,
Will abide.

So the pain thy soul sustaineth,
Endeth soon, thy chastening o'er;
But the beauty He engraineth,
And the grace thy spirit gaineth
In thine hour of grief, remaineth
Evermore.

# The Ploughman

1 Chron. 15. 36

N AY, call not Death 'the Reaper!' Not the scythe, the
plough
Is all he holds. Though in his sombre furrow now
The precious grain must fall, and pass, decayed from sight,
'Tis but the seed-time yet; bide thou the harvest bright!

Then shalt thou see a Reaper, different far, appear,
And from each teeming furrow glean the mellowed ear.
Triumphant, glorious, glad, He bears His harvest home,
Come, Day of Joy undimmed! Blest Reaper, quickly come!

# Restoration

*Lo, the winter is past, the rain is over and gone; the flowers*
*appear on the earth; the time of singing is come.*
— Song of Sol. 2. 11-12

M Y heart was like a winter's field, barren and dead.
Then came a day when all the sky o'erhead
Grew dark with cloud and tempest, and the rain
Swept pitiless across that frigid plain.

'Tis past; and, lo, with springtide's lovely green
Arrayed afresh, the sunlit sward is seen.
Fragrant and fair the flowers of God appear,
And notes of heavenly music greet the ear.

I bless Thee, O my Father, for Thy rains —
The losses, sorrows, disappointments, pains —
Sent from Thy treasuries, in mercy true,
To make a selfish heart grow soft, and bloom anew.

# The Legacy

*The holy garments of Aaron shall be his sons' after him.* —
Exod. 29. 29

WHAT shall he leave his sons? Silver nor gold,
   Nor heritage, has he, nor herd nor fold.
Not these can he bequeath, but this he can —
The holy raiment of a saintly man.

The fair example of a life well spent;
Of daily tendance in the sacred Tent;
Of ever-praiseful heart and reverent mind;
What nobler gift could father leave behind?

That son who, drawing near the Throne of Grace,
Can say, "How well my father knew this Place!
How oft I've heard his voice in fervent prayer!"
Happy that son, that richly-dowered heir.

# The Innocents

(Compare Matt. 2. 17-18 with Jer. 31. 15-17)

A VOICE was heard in Ramah, bitter mourning, lamentation;
   Rachel weeping for her children; who can render consolation?
Who can wipe that burning tear,
   Who can hush that bitter cry?
O why leave the mother here,
   If the little one must die?

A voice was heard from Heaven, "Stay thy tears, restrain thy
weeping.
They shall come again, thy dear ones, from the far land of their
      sleeping."
   At thine end, sweet Hope is left,
      Best reward for sorest pain;
   To the heart whence they were reft,
      Mother, they shall come again!

# If the Lord Will

*We will go into such a city, and continue there (residence),
and buy and sell (occupation), and get gain (income). Ye
ought to say, If the Lord will.* — James 4. 13-15

WHERE I shall dwell, what toil my days employ,
    And whether I shall gain thereby or lose,
Are not, O Lord, for me to will and choose.
The will, the choice, are Thine, I own with joy.

To-morrow's lot I know not, nor can tell
    How soon this vapour, Life, shall flit from sight.
    I only know Thy will is ever right,
Thy child can trust: Thou doest all things well.


# As this Little Child

Matt. 18. 4

AH, gracious Lord, Thou knowest I would fain
    Thy sweet behest in very deed obey;
    Fling all this pride and strife and care away,
And gladly be a little child again.
Alas, I cannot. Well I know, with pain,
    The Dawn is past — for ever past and gone.
    Noontide is here, and Night will come anon.

I shall not, can not, be a child again.
    Yet well I know, O Lord, Thy lips all-wise
Framed never yet a mocking word or vain.
    Anoint with salve, I pray Thee, these dim eyes,
That I may read Thy lovely meaning plain.
    Let me be humble, loving, trustful, free from guile or guise;
So only shall I be a child again.

# All

*The Request — Drink ye all of it. —* Matt. 26. 27

*The Response — They all drank of it. —* Mark 14. 23

'WOULD He, then, miss me if I did not come?'
    While one is absent, then He hath not all.
'Lacks He His portion if my heart is dumb?'
    The whole requires each part, howe'er so small.

'All,' Love demands; and love respondeth, 'All!'
    When there's a praiseless heart, a vacant seat,
A chord is lacking; and the strains that fall
    Upon the listening Ear are incomplete.

# The Apple Tree

*As the apple tree among the trees of the wood, so is my
Beloved among the sons. —* Song of Sol. 2. 3

THE Apple tree, among the forest trees,
    Strikes down its roots into the self-same ground,
Shares the same dews with all the trees around;
Its leaves are rustled by the self-same breeze.
Yet is it of a nature not like these.
    A foliage different from the rest it wears,
    A fruit peculiar to itself it bears:
So is the Apple tree among the trees.

And so among the sons is my Beloved.
    True Man indeed, with all man's feelings, He;
And as amongst us in and out He moved,
    Was tempted in all matters like as we.
Yet sinless ever, and by God approved,
    He stands unique in lovely purity.

# The Mirror

*Clearly seen . . . by the things that are made.* — Rom. 1. 20

THE Sunbeam shimmering o'er the sea,
    The Lily blooming on the lea,
Tell of His light and purity.

The Lamb, the Lion and the Roe,
The Stream, the Cloud, the shining Bow,
His manifold perfections show.

The soaring Eagle's sweep above,
The gentle cooing of the Dove,
Proclaim His might and croon His love.

The bruised Grape, the Corn of Wheat,
The mystic parable repeat
His blood and flesh my drink and meat.

The Lightning's blaze, out-flashing far,
The beam serene of Morning Star,
The prophets of His advent are.

Look where thou wilt, thine eye may trace
In lovely tint and form of grace,
Some mirrored feature of His face.

# When God Demands

*Fetch me water,*
*Bring me bread,*
*Give me thy son.* — 1 Kings 17. 10, 11, 19

**M** YSTERIOUS and dark are oft the ways
Whereby our God His tender love displays.

In tones abrupt the rugged seer demands
Her one last handful from the widow's hands.
A hard request? So unbelief would say:
Faith meekly hears and boldly dares obey.
And since she thus her all does not refuse,
God gives her the unwasting meal, the unfailing cruse.

She knew the sting of poverty: a son
To care for, when the meal and oil were done.
She now has plenty; but what's all her store
If death has seized on him she loved far more?
However hard may be "Give me thy Bread",
"Give me thy Son!" is mandate for more dread.
Who would not sooner see the meal-barrel spent
Than weep a broken-hearted Rachel's long lament?

But O the grace of God! Would we had eyes
Rightly to view His providences wise!
He never takes but that He may restore,
Made tenfold precious, all we had before.
Her prospect once was but to "eat and die";
"See, thy son liveth" now she hears the prophet cry.

Thus on the place of emptiness and death
Does God oft breathe; and though at first His breath
Seems but to blast and wither everything,
Soon thou shalt see new life and new abundance spring.

# Caligraphy

*I will write upon him.* — Rev. 3. 12

T IME writes; his busy, prodding pencil, Care,
Touches the brow, and leaves a sentence there.

Pride writes; on haughty lip and lofty eye,
All may the tell-tale characters descry.

Hate writes; Lust writes. All vices leave their trace,
Brand-marks of Satan, on the human face.

Blest Lord, Thou writest, too! Write on me, then,
With Thy dear hand, though pain should be Thy pen,
And tears Thy ink. Spell on my face, my heart,
Some syllable to tell how good Thou art.

# Love's Cipher

*Jonathan went out into the field at the time appointed with David, and . . . shot an arrow.* — 1 Sam. 20. 35-36

A WASTED shaft, shot idly in the air
So may the world's wisdom deem thy prayer.
The unseen Watcher marks thy arrow's flight;
He knows its language, reads its message right.

He joys, because thy love has kept His tryst;
Deep joy is thine, communing with the Christ.
The world that cast Him out can never know
The secret art of talking with Him so.
They see His seat is empty; men of prayer
Know where He is, and how to find Him there.

# The Sabbath-Breaker

*They found a man that gathered sticks upon the Sabbath Day.* — Numbers 15. 32

H E is not hewing in the wood,
　　Nor mining in the hill;
He is not ploughing in the field,
　　Nor grinding at the mill.
It is not nuggets from the sands,
　　But trifles that he picks.
He is not doing something great,
　　But simply "gathering sticks".
Thus often not the heaviest cares
　　Of life, not sharpest woes,
But little fears and little frets,
　　Disturbs the soul's repose.
We let such paltry, trivial things
　　Our peace of mind unfix:
We mar and break our Sabbath rest
　　To worry over — sticks!

# An Assembly Fable

S AID the Telegraph Pole to the Tree,
　　"Why don't you have branches like me,
"All sawn and all spaced, all measured and placed
　　"As even and straight as can be."

Said the Tree to the Telegraph Pole
　　"I think I'd prefer, on the whole,
"That my branches still grew, just as God meant them to,
　　"Springing out of not nailed to my bole."

Every fable a moral must show
　　Alive, though diverse let us grow,
From the one common root, bearing each his own fruit,
　　Not just telegraph poles in a row.

# The Greatest, the Least

*These shall first set forth.* — Numbers 2. 9

*They shall go hindmost.* — Numbers 2. 31

WHEN from the Tent the Cloudy Pillar rose,
Sign that another journey must begin,
The watchful priest the silver trumpet blows,
The camp moves on in godly discipline.
The hosts of Judah boldly lead the van
Last with their standards come the tribes of Dan.

Each takes the place appointed, high or low,
And each is needed in the place assigned,
Some are required in front to face the foe
Some tribe must fill the humble post behind.
None can be spared: for God's symmetric plan
Calls both for Judah's work and that of Dan.

So likewise is there in the Church today
A twofold need — for courage, and for grace.
Courage to bear the brunt and lead the way,
Meekness to take the lowest, hindmost place,
He only is a throughly furnished man,
Who is at once a Judah and a Dan.

Thus, if reproach and danger must be met,
The chiefest of apostles then is Paul.
In furthering the Truth he leads; and yet
Among the saints he is the least of all.
A babe in malice though in mind a man;
In service Judah, but in boasting, Dan.

# Dead Lions

*A living dog is better than a dead lion.* — Eccles. 9. 4

" **A** LIVING dog," the Wise Man said,
"Is better than a lion dead."
What's giant frame or royal mien,
Where life itself no more is seen?

And so with preachers. All in vain
Are showy gifts and powerful brain.
Unless His might the spirit gives;
Unless, in short, the Lion lives!

I'd rather hear the halting speech,
Of humblest, puniest men that preach,
If through their homely phrases shine
The evidence of life Divine.


# In His Temple

*Open flowers.* — 1 Kings 6. 18

**M** UCH here is in the bud. Not yet revealed,
The heavenly hues, within dark sheaths concealed,
Wait still the sunshine at "That Day" to share.
The bud is here; the opened flower is There.

Here are the falling leaves, the shattered bloom,
Autumn of slow decay, then winters doom;
But yonder in His temple, ever fair
From year to year, the full-bloomed flower is There.

Now, immature, then we shall be "like Him";
Then glory-bright, though tarnished now and dim.
Wonder of grace, we shall His likeness wear,
Mature, yet fading not. O to be There!

# SALT AND SEASONING

# Barley Cakes

THE Midianite is in the land,
    And Israel's hard bestead.
There's poverty on every hand,
    And scarcity of bread:
But brawny Gideon beats at night
    The threshing of his floor,
And by the winepress, out of sight,
    Conceals his precious store.

How well his honest heart esteems
    The food his God has given!
A plain unleavened cake he deems
    Fit for a guest from Heaven.
Here is a man whom God can tell,
    'Go thou in this thy might.'
Yes, Midian's tents shall prove how well
    A 'barley cake' can fight!

A lesson learn from Gideon's floor:
    Nutritious food for you
Is in the Word; abundance more
    Than ever Caanan grew.
And if you wish to serve the Lord
    (For still His foes assail),
If you would learn to use the Sword,
    First learn to use the Flail!

# I Wonder

*Whose adorning let it not be that outward adorning of
plaiting the hair, and wearing of gold, or putting on of
apparel; but let it be the hidden man of the heart . . . a
meek and quiet spirit, which is in the sight of God of great
price.* — 1 Pet. 3. 3-4

I WONDER just how we'd be dressed,
If you and I, and all the rest,
To-morrow morn a garment donned
That should exactly correspond
To what makes up, as best it can,
The wardrobe of our 'hidden man'?

Yon mincing beauty, tripping by,
The cynosure of every eye;
What if, for once, she had to part
With jeweller's and tailor's art,
And substituted for the whole,
Such scarecrow rags as drape the soul?

What if yon Dives, pompous, vain,
Shed his broadcloth and golden chain,
And, outward, as within, was seen
Naked and poor, and blind, and mean?
The beggar at his gate might be
Far better dressed, perhaps, than he.

And what if I . . .? Yes, it is true,
*That* question must be answered, too!
So now before this faithful glass
(The Word of Truth) an hour I'll pass,
In its unflattering depths to scan
How I've adorned my 'hidden man.'

# Honey and Brass

*Thou shalt eat . . .*
*Thou mayest dig . . .* — Deut. 8. 9

'TIS a good land and large that thy God has bestowed,
    Aflow with its fountains and rills.
With sheaves and with clusters the valleys are strowed,
    There's iron and brass in the hills.

Thy oil and thy honey are free as the air
    In ease and content thou may'st dwell;
But before the *full* wealth of the Land thou can'st share,
    Thou must needs be a miner as well!

A stranger may gather a grape or a fig,
    A spy bear a cluster away;
But if down to the ore in the rock thou would'st dig,
    Thou must dwell in the Land every day.


# Our Difficulties

(cf. 1 Chron. 11. 22 and Prov. 26. 13-14)

THERE'S many a sluggard turns his drowsy head
    To talk of 'lions' from a downy bed.
But, lack-alas! the fierce old beasts of prey
Are seldom hunted on the 'snowy day.'

A man of words may tell you how to meet
Imaginary lions in the street;
But when you find the live one in his lair,
It takes a man of might to beard him there!

37

# The Stars Also

Gen. 1. 16

H E made the sun that day by day
　　Pours down its radiance bright.
He made yon stately moon that rules
　　In silvery pomp the night.
But all those tiny twinkling specks
　　As far as eye can go,
I watch with wonder when I think,
　　'He made the stars also.'

But I am glad; because, you see,
　　My life so small appears —
Not big and brilliant like the sun
　　That lights the rolling years,
Nor fair and lovely like the moon.
　　I'm just a speck, I know.
Yet He who made those greater lights,
　　'He made the stars also.'

Then, there are things in daily life
　　That seem so mean and slight,
We wonder, does God really keep
　　Such tiny things in sight?
But now I know however small
　　Those little things may show,
They'll not escape His loving eye,
　　Who 'made the stars also.'

But *are* they small, those twinkling specks?
　　Or should I maybe find
(Had I the eyes) each one exceed
　　Both sun and moon combined?
And — who can tell — those things that men
　　Deem 'weak' and 'base' and low,
May be the greatest things with Him
　　Who 'made the stars also.'

# The Raven

*Consider the ravens . . . God feedeth them.* — Luke 12. 24

I have commanded the ravens to feed thee. — 1 Kings 17. 4

I 'M neither nightingale nor lark,
    I neither soar nor sing;
A sombre bird of plumage dark,
    Ungraceful on the wing.
I have, I fear, a croaking voice;
    My use is hard to see.
'Tis all too true! yet I rejoice;
    For why? God feedeth me!

He loves this all unlovely me.
    He hears my cry; He cares.
He knows me at my worst, yet He
    For all my need prepares.
He knows my worthlessness, yet still
    At times His grace may choose,
For bearing errands at His will,
    My useless self to use.

So if I know no tuneful song,
    I'll croak as best I may.
If I can't soar, I'll flap along
    My own old usual way.
If to some needier one I can
    Some timely succour bring,
I've been *some* use to God and man:
    Is that not everything?

# Suppositions

*Supposing Him to be in the company. — Luke 2. 44*

*Supposing Him to be the gardener. — John 20. 15*

T HEY did not miss Him. Ah, they knew it not
    That He was absent, or they had forgot.
They careless thought that near them He had been,
Yet all a "three days" distance lay between!

How Mary missed Him! Ah, she knew too well
The Lord was absent, and those weepings tell.
How deep her longing to behold the Face
Which not an angel's brightness could replace.

They missed Him not, so He remained behind,
She missed and sought Him, and who seeks shall find.
'Tis when we've learned His absence, He's revealed,
If we "suppose" Him here, He's still concealed.

# Testing and Teaching

*The devil taketh Him up into an exceeding high mountain.*
*— Matt. 4. 8*

*He went up into a mountain, opened His mouth and taught.*
*— Matt. 5. 1-2*

W OULD'ST thou teach others? There is need,
    But ponder well the thought —
Thy Lord Himself, the living Truth,
    First *practised,* then He *taught.*
Think not to climb where Jesus sat
    In moral elevation,
Till, like Him, you've triumphant left
    The mountain of temptation.

Dare one exhort, "For food, for drink,
    For raiment, have no care,"
Who ne'er himself a desert trod,
    Fasting, yet trusting, there?
None may with power divine unfold
    The Heavenly Kingdom's story,
Save those who've scorned the kingdoms of
    This world, and all their glory.

# Smitten of God

NAY, child of God! Dost thou repine,
    And mourn a stroke that seems so sore?
Hush! 'Tis the touch of Love Divine
    Has reached thee, low on dungeon floor.
Know if thy Father smiteth thee,
'Tis but to rouse and set thee free
To blest unfettered liberty.

But thou, proud sinner, howsoe'er
    The world may fawn, applaud, and crown
And set thee up on high: beware!
    From thence my God can bring thee down.
Ah! from His stroke of judgement dread,
Fierce anger and damnation red,
What shield can fence they guilty head!

# The Other Four

YOUNG David chose five smooth stones from the brook.
    To slay Goliath just one stone he took.
So he who seemed so ill-equipped before,
Has weapons now enough, and four times more.

Thus is it ever; God's resources still
Surpass the needs of all who wait His will.
Nor when His last proud foe is overthrown,
Will half His strength exhaustless yet be known.

# Your Shadow

*They even carried out the sick into the streets . . . that, as
Peter came by, at least his shadow might overshadow some
one of them. — Acts 5. 15*

A S Peter's shadow seemed to cast
    A blessing wheresoe'er he passed;
So to thy life an influence clings,
That either good or evil brings.
Are men the better, then, I pray,
When falls thy "shadow" on their way?

# The End of the Lord

*How long shall it be to the end? — Dan. 12.6*

*What shall be the end? — Dan. 12. 8*

*Go thy way till the end . . . thou shall stand in thy lot at
the end. — Dan. 12. 13*

T HE time seemed long, "When shall it be,
    The end of strife and pain and
        tragedy?"
*Go thou thy way, thy trusting heart at rest,
God's time, how long so e'er, is always best.*

The days were dark. "Ah, to what end
(If end there be) do life's sad mysteries tend?"
*Go then thy way undoubting; thou shall see
God's end will justify His ways with thee.*

"But Lord, I prayed that yon fair plot
In Judah's land be my appointed lot."
*Go thou thy way content. Not here, but There,
See, waiting thee, God's answer to thy prayer.*

# Dedicated or Dissipated?

*They presented unto Him . . . gold.* — Matt. 2. 11

*They gave large money unto the soldiers.* — Matt. 28. 12

WE read of some who, from a distant land,
　　Their treasures brought to Christ, with homage due.
We read of those who spent with lavish hand,
　　To drown a truth they dared not own as true.
'Tis not for nought that thou these things are told . . .
How spendest thou, my friend, thy silver and thy gold?

Note: It is interesting to observe how much Matthew, "the publican", has to say regarding the use of money. He is the only one of the four Evangelists to mention the two incidents alluded to above.

# Election, Faith and Works

*Salmon begat Boaz of Rahab.* — Matt. 1. 5

*By faith the harlot Rahab perished not.* — Heb. 11. 31

*Was not Rahab the harlot justified by works?* — Jas. 2. 25

GRACE spared the harlot Rahab's life,
　　Grace made her Salmon's virtuous wife.
So from the dust she's raised to shine
'Mong princes of the Royal line.

All was of grace; and yet by *Faith*
She perished not, the Scripture saith.
For what electing grace intends,
Faith, freely choosing, apprehends.

By grace through faith — 'tis very meet:
Add one link more, the chain's complete,
By *Works* must Rahab's faith be sealed,
Ere all God's purpose stands revealed.

# The Widening Circle

I N but one sequence will the Truth
   Divinely operate —
'Tis first the *heart,* and then the *home,*
   And last the *outer gate.*

Religion all inscribed without,
   For passers-by to see,
But never round the fireside shown,
   Were sorry sanctity.
And "idle tales" your talk would seem
   To those with whom you dwelt,
If well they knew the truth you taught,
   Was truth you never felt.

But light, thine own soul flooding first,
   Will soon thy dwelling fill.
Then shining from thy portals far,
   Reach circles wider still.


# Master, Speak

"S PEAK to my sister!" "Speak to my brother!"
   Unhappy, if such be thy plea,
Whilst He whom thou prayest to speak to another,
   Has somewhat to say unto thee!

# The Idol Maker

*That it may remain in the house.* — Isaiah 44. 13

What doeth he,
Who, late and early, toils so busily?
See how he deftly plies each suited tool —
Axe, saw and plane the compasses, the rule!
With practised hand, so skilfully,
What maketh he? What maketh he?

Wait yet awhile,
That thing his inmost chamber shall defile;
Shall sit enthronéd there; bear baneful sway
O'er all his thoughts and actions all the day.
Yea, follow him, an ever-present blight,
To taint the very slumbers of the night.
No more to God who made him does he bow:
The thing his own hands made he worships now.

Alas, O God, that any man should take
The strength and skill Thou givest, and should make
Nought for Thy glory or Thy creatures' good,
But some abomination gross as yonder.
                    god of wood!

# A Word to the Silent Brothers

James 1. 19-26

**B**E slow to speak; but don't be *dumb!*
      God wants you to be able
To put a bridle on your tongue —
      Not lock it in the stable!

# Requiscat in pace

FATHER, Thy child is tired, and fain would rest
    In that still, tranquil bed, where Thou dost lay
Thy loved to sleep. No more pursued, distressed,
    By all the throng and clamour of the day;
No more to feel rebellious passions sway
    My wayward heart from following the best;
No more of baffled quest and doubtful fray;
    O it were good in your calm bed to rest!

But if not yet awhile the sunset blest
    Must throw its welcome shadow on my way;
With noonday's heat and burdens still oppressed,
    I cry to Thee; O hear me as I pray —
"Outspread Thy wing, and from the burning ray
    Teach me to shelter, safe and undistressed
The grave he need not covet, who can say
    His rest, his shelter, is the Saviour's breast."

# Trivialities

TO strain the gnats; to strive o'er words;
    To tithe the mint and rue;
No tasks are those for helpful hands
    And fervent hearts to do.

Forbid it, that when I am gone,
    My epitaph should be —
"According to our straitest sect
    He lived — a pharisee."

# Vineyard-Keeping

*They made me the keeper of the vineyards; but mine own vineyard have I not kept.* — Song of So. 1. 6

**B**USY running to and fro,
　Busy toiling here and there;
Not an idle hour to show,
　Not a minute left to spare.

To every call a ready ear,
　For every task a hand adept;
But one thing's left undone, I fear —
　"My own vineyard I have not kept."

I would not slow the busy pace,
　I would not stay the helpful hands;
Nor would I, with averted face,
　Pass by when need my help demands.

But teach me, Lord (for was Thou not
　The busiest, yet the holiest Man?)
How first to tend my private plot,
　Then haste to do what else I can.

# Within and Without

Ps. 133. 2, 3

**L**IKE holy ointment, filty blending;
　Like dew from heaven, soft descending;
The ungrieved Spirit leads us in,
As holy priests, the veil within;
Or, as we fare to hills without,
Distils His grace our path about.

Priesthood and service, shrine and hill,
Need dew and heavenly unction still;
And still His blessing He commands
On loving hearts, united hands.
How good, how pleasant, past all telling!
God dwells with those in union dwelling.

# Spiritual Posture

*Upon my face.* — Ezek. 1. 28 & 3. 23

*Upon my feet.* — Ezek. 2. 2 & 3. 24

"UPON my face," to worship low before Him;
    "Upon my feet," alert His will to do;
They serve Him best whose spirits most adore Him;
They worship best, who will to serve Him too.

# SEEDLINGS

# The Unclean Birds

*The screech-owl also shall rest there, and find for herself a place of rest. There shall the great owl make her nest, and lay, and hatch, and gather under her shadow: there shall the vultures also be gathered every one with her mate.*
— Isaiah 34. 14-15

'**E**ACH one her mate!' Alas, it is too true,
Each sin allowed within the heart to rest
Brings its companion-sin, and thus with new
And yet more foul pollution fills the breast.

Nor is there any end: for constantly
(As owls their loathsome broods industrious rear)
Sin hatches sin, a hateful progeny,
Increasing day by day and year by year.

# The Wicker Basket

*The birds did eat them out of the basket upon my head.* —
Gen. 40. 17

Beware!
**T**HOU art a steward; thou dost bear
Thy Master's property. O have a care
Lest, fell and swift, like as the birds of air,
His foes swoop down, and e'er thou art
aware,
Have left thy basket bare.

# Response

*Unto you.* — Rev. 1. 4

*Unto Him.* — Rev. 1. 5

U NTO us the blessings,
    Unto Him the praise.
His to send the mercies,
    Ours the song to raise.
He hath loved us, loosed us,
    Made us priests to be;
His be all the glory
    Through eternity.

# The Two Signs

*Jesus was called to the marriage . . . This beginning of
miracles did Jesus.* — John 2. 2-11

*Come down ere my child die . . . This is the second miracle
that Jesus did.* — John 4. 49-54

W HERE happy hearts are lightest,
    Lo, He's there.
In joy the fullest, brightest,
    He can share.

When sorrows press severest,
    Still the same,
He's nearer than the nearest,
    Bless His Name!

# The Two Wonders

*He marvelled . . . so great faith.* — Matt. 8. 10

*He marvelled because of their unbelief.* — Mark 6. 6

T HERE are two marvels which outvie
    All other wonders 'neath the sky;
A faith that seeth but the clearer
As gathering trials press severer;
An unbelief that grows more blind,
The more God shows His mercies kind.

# At the Cock-Crowing

*And immediately the cock crew. — John 18. 27*

" 'TIS night, but dawn is near;
      The Day will soon be here.
Then every deed in darkness wrought,
Each sinful word, each shameful thought,
      Naked and plain and clear,
      Shall in the light appear.
O let my clarion keen awake thee
Lest as a thief that Day o'ertake thee!"
      Thus to the conscience-quickened ear
      The cock-crow calleth clear.


# In Training

*It was that Mary which anointed the Lord with ointment,
and wiped His feet with her hair, whose brother Lazarus was
sick. — John 11. 2*

IN Sorrow's school is worship taught the best, for there
    To Faith's submissive ear this truth is spoken:
'The heart, an alabaster box of ointment rare,
Yields most when broken.'


# Wings

*O that I had wings like a dove; then would I fly away and be
at rest. — Psa. 55. 6*

*They that wait upon the Lord . . . shall mount up with
wings as eagles. — Isaiah 40. 31*

I FAIN would fly and leave my cares behind,
    But how or where to flee I cannot find.
Seems then a voice to say — "Tis better so:
Learn thou to *soar* and leave thy cares *below!'*

# Which?

*In the sight of God.* — 2 Cor. 2. 17

*In the sight of men.* — Rev. 13. 13

WHEN thou art following Christ, the lowly One,
All that thou dost as in God's sight is done.
But when thy works are for the sight of men,
'Tis Antichrist's proud spirit rules thee then.

# The Condemnation

*Inasmuch as ye did it not.* — Matt. 25. 45

O WEIGH thou well His judgment just and true:
(The thronéd Son, shall He not judge aright?)
The greatest evil any man can do,
Is not to do the little good he might.

# Wilderness

*He was with the wild beats; and the angels ministered unto Him.* — Mark 1. 13

EARTH hath no wilderness so grim and bare,
Or so with savage fangs beset around,
But for the soul that trusteth shall be found
Some tender heavenly ministration there.

# Minutiæ

*Handkerchiefs and aprons* — Acts 19.12

*Loaves and fishes.* — John 6. 9

*Bridles and pots.* — Zech 14. 20

THE tiniest thing
To Him thou mayest bring.
Blessed by His sanctifying touch
The least is much.

# The Test

W ITH wealth would'st be blessed?
'Tis a man's hardest test.
Unless it is shared,
He's snared!

# Equipoise

*Take heed. — Mark 13. 9*

*Take no thought. — Mark 13. 11*

" T AKE heed! Beware,
Yet be thou free from care!''
Teach me, O Lord, amid life's strain and noise,
To keep this balanced mien, this happy poise;
Tranquil, though vigilant, to be;
Not careless, but carefree.

# I Must Decrease

*I am not the Christ. — John 1. 20*

*I am not . . . no. — John 1.21*

C ARELESS of human praise or blame
Eschewing self-display;
The more men asked him of himself
The less he had to say.

# Spiritual Sequence

*The disciples went, and did as Jesus appointed them. —*
*Matt. 21. 6*

*And they . . . found even as He had said. —* Luke 19. 32

*The disciples did as Jesus had appointed them.*
*— Matt. 26. 19*

*And they . . . found as He had said. —* Luke 22. 13

'TIS true from ancient days
Tis true till Time be sped,
That those who do as Jesus says
Shall find as Jesus said.

# The Door and the Window

*When thou prayest . . . shut thy door. —* Matt. 6. 6

*His windows being open . . . he prayed. —* Dan. 6. 10

THERE is a Door whence man, from day to day,
Steps out to tread the streets of Babylone;
There is a Window, too, that looks away,
To God's fair city, to Jehovah's Throne.
There is a time to use the Door, 'tis true,
But when thou prayest, if thou would'st be heard,
To God, not to thy fellows, turn thy view,
Thy window open, but thy Door fast barred.

# Kingdom of Earth — Kingdom of Heaven

*Nimrod — a mighty one in the earth — the beginning of his*
*kingdom was Babel. —* Gen. 10. 8-10

*Let us build a tower whose top may reach to Heaven. —*
Gen. 11. 4

*Children . . . of such is the kingdom of Heaven. —* Matt. 19. 14

IN vain the great ones of the earth may try
To found on earth a tower to reach the sky.
God takes the lowliest child of heavenly birth,
To bring the rule of heaven down to earth.

# Feeble yet Necessary

*The king himself is served by the field.* — Ecc. 5. 9

T HE lowly worm, with toil unseen,
    Keeps all the verdant valley green.
There graze the herds; and they, again,
Do man, creation's head, sustain.

Hence learn a lesson good to know —
Let none despise his brother low.
The chief, though ne'er so great increased,
Is still dependent on the least.

# Why Not?

I F all with whom we had to do
    Were kind and courteous, fair and true;
How much more pleasant it would be
For everybody, you'll agree.
All *are* not so? No, that is true;
But any *may*, . . . so why not you?

# Continuance

*All the time.* — Acts. 1. 21

N OT only in the sunshine's ray,
    Not only while you get your way;
Not a disciple for a day,
    But "all the time."

If post of trust you'd ever fill,
There's just one way; keep plodding still,
On, on, through good report and ill,
    Yes, "all the time."

# Predestination

TOO late, ye hosts of darkness!
    Ye cannot work me ill.
Before your plots, His promise,
    Before your oath, His will.

His wisdom ere your cunning,
    His love forestalls your hate.
Begone, ye hosts of darkness,
    Your schemes are far too late!

# "A Body of its Own"

THEY were not all alike when they were here.
    Some sprightly, some were grave; some gentle, mild;
Some strong with fiery might for conflicts wild.
So different all, yet each how very dear!

They are not all alike now they are There,
Loosed from the cumbering flesh. See, even now,
The starry splendour that bedecks the brow
Differs in each, though all so heavenly fair.

# Stilled — Filled — Skilled

I WOULD be *stilled;* each clamouring care
Brought to His holy calm, and silenced there.

I would be *filled;* with love, with power,
Yea, all the Spirit's fulness, heavenly dower.

I would be *skilled;* to know, to do
Whatever things are pure and kind and true.

# As thy Days

*Two days.* John 11. 6

*Two pence.* — Luke 10. 35

THE Lord is absent; still our eyes must weep,
The loving sorrow, and the loved ones sleep.
We look, we long, but He doth not appear.
Still sighs the burdened heart, "O that He had been here!"

The Lord is absent. Yes, but not His grace!
His care, His riches, bless my wayside place
With all I need. Till He return for me,
E'en as my days, I know, will His provision be.

# Divine Architecture

*The upper chambers were shorter . . . straitened more than
the lowest and middlemost.* — Ezekiel 42. 5-6

AND dost thou fret because this niche confined
Is all the Architect to thee assigned?
Patience! His plan is just and kind and wise —
The staitest rooms are nearest to the skies!

# Alpha and Omega

I T was the morn of Time; but man had need
    Of peace and pardon; so the lamb must bleed.

And now the evening falls on Time's long day.
Much man has done and learned along his way;
But still in need the burdened spirit cries
At even, as at morn, for sacrifice.
And still this only cure for sin I see —
The Lamb upon the Altar, slain for me.

# Incense

S EE in what divers ways, before the Throne,
    The heavenly hosts their sinless worship pour!
(The lowly posture, the triumphant tone,
    Be thine today, as theirs for evermore).

The gladsome song: the voice of spoken praise
    From lips sincere: the brief, heartfelt "Amen":
The voiceless soul's adoring: all upraise
    Sweet incense from the Altar, now as then.

# The Pitcher

*Phil. 4. 19 R.V.*

O little could I draw, or bear
    Away from yonder spring,
If ne'er an empty pitcher there
    Had I to bring.

And little should I know, indeed,
    His glorious fulness still
If I had ne'er a hungry need
    For Him to fill.

# Request and Behest

Luke 22. 19        John 21. 19

"REMEMBER Me," the Saviour said;
    And still, responsive to His word,
We drink the wine, we break the bread,
    In fond remembrance of the Lord.

"Come, follow Me," the Saviour said;
    And rising, we would follow still;
At home, abroad, at toil and trade,
    The prompt disciples of His will.

# Man speaks to God

Gen. 3. 9          Rev. 22. 20

A SHAMED before his Maker, filled with dread;
  Guilt and disgrace on his dishonoured head;
Man speaks to God — "I heard thy voice," saith he
"And being naked, feared, and hid from Thee."

Joyful before his Saviour, blessed through grace,
Man lifts to Heaven a longing, loving face.
The voice Divine he hears: with kindling eyes,
"Come, even so, Lord Jesus!" he replies.

See how the sacred Scriptures thus contrast
Man's first recorded speech to God, and last.
Think then how hot the Altar coal had been,
Whose touch could make such unclean lips so clean.

# The Touchstone

*The Shepherds came with haste.* — Luke 2. 16

*They that fed the swine . . . fled.* — Luke 8. 34

T HE Shepherds feared, but still drew nigh;
  The swineherds feared and fled.
Do thou the touchstone still apply —
  Prove in His presence dread,
By what may stand and what must fly,
  The clean or unclean trade.
What cannot bear His holy eye
  Were better drowned and dead.

# His Majesty

*Eyewitnesses of His majesty . . . on the Holy Mount.*
— 2 Pet. 1. 16-18

*They were all amazed at the majesty of God.* — Luke 9. 43

MAJESTIC on the Holy Mount; so bright
   The favoured three His glories scarce may scan;
While visitors august, from realms of light,
   Hold reverent discourse with the Son of Man.

The scene below how sordid! Sin and strife,
   Disease and demon power, their ranks have ranged,
Yet still He moves serene, the Prince of Life,
   Majestic still, though all things else were changed.

# Very Early

*When it was yet dark.* — John 20. 1

*As it began to dawn.* — Matt. 28. 1

*At the rising of the sun.* — Mark 16. 2

IT yet was dark; but Love can find her way
   (Sure-footed Love!) by night as well as day.

The first soft trace of dawn. Hope's eager eye
Marks every hue that tints the eastern sky.

Sunrise at last! Faith's sure reward is here;
Death turned to life; black night to morning clear.

# Work and Rest

*I have filled him with the Spirit . . . to work.* — Ex. 31. 3-4

*The sabbath of rest.* — Ex. 31. 15

O may Thy Spirit teach my hands to toil,
Lest I be idle, or, unskilled, should spoil
With witless haste the task ordained to me.
O teach me how to work, and work with Thee.

O may Thy Spirit teach my heart to rest;
Tranquil to share with Thee Thy sabbath blest;
Resting from all my work and want and care,
Resting in Christ, for Thou art resting there.

# The Christian's Ambition

FOR Him to toil, with Him to walk, in Him to live,
By Him to war, from Him to draw, to Him to give;
Of Him to speak, through Him to praise; like Him to be
On Him to feast, now and eternally.

# Praise

*"Hearest thou what these say?" Jesus saith, "Yea."*
— Matt. 21. 16

AH, pause thou, my soul, and remember,
Ere thou with thy tribute draw near;
It was to the song of the children
The Saviour was pleased to give ear.
"The mouths of the babes and the sucklings,"
How artless and simple their lays.
Yet this is acceptable worship,
Yea, this is perfection of praise.

# True Perspective

Phil. 4. 6, 7

**M**AYHAPS thy heart is still oppressed
With yesterday's sore sorrow
Thy mind with anxious care distressed
For what shall be tomorrow.
Make known to Him thy case; and thou shall find
The peace of God possess both heart and mind.

# Another Day!

**A**NOTHER debt I never can repay.
Not all the gold of Ophir could have bought
Thy sunshine or Thy air: I gave Thee nought.

# Night and Day

*That Day. — Mark 14. 25*

*This Night. — Mark 14. 30*

"**T**HIS night," . . . "That day!"
O give me grace, I pray,
So in the darkness to be true to Thee,
That when at last the rising dawn I see,
"That Day" shall seem more bright,
Because I knew "This Night."

# Substitution

*In Christ's stead. — 2 Cor. 5.20*

*In our stead. — 2 Cor. 5.21*

**M**ADE sin upon the shameful Tree
He died, a substitute for thee
Let this be then thy prayer, thy aim
To live a substitute for Him.

# SONGS

# Advent Anthem

TELL the story of the Saviour, how from highest
    Heaven He came,
With His hands all filled with blessing and His heart with
    love aflame.
Tell the sorrows of His Passion, show the mysteries of the
    Tree,
Preach Him risen, crowned and seated, none with higher
    Name than He.

Spread the message of redemption wheresoever man, in
    chains,
Feels the bitterness of bondage, knows the vileness of his
    stains,
Tell of  power to raise the helpless, tell of vision for the
    blind,
Tell of uttermost salvation for the neediest of mankind.

Let the Herald's trump be sounding for the coming of the
    King;
Mid the world's perplexed confusion let the proclamation
    ring —
Lift your heads, all ye who love Him; bow, ye rebel
    sinners, bow,
For the Christ doth come in Glory — He is on the
    threshold now.

# The Song of Moses

Exodus 15

I will sing unto the Lord,
  He hath triumphed gloriously.
Horse and rider, spear and sword,
  He hath cast into the sea;
Hosts and chariots overthrown,
His the glory, His alone.

He my strength and He my song,
  He my sure salvation is.
Let Him dwell His saints among,
  Let the praise be ever His.
Sing, O Israel, thou art free,
He hath triumphed gloriously.

Glorious is Thy hand in might,
  Fierce Thy wrath, Thy mercy kind,
Thou Thy ransomed lead'st aright,
  Guide and guard in Thee they find.
Feared and honoured who should be,
Wonder-working God, like Thee?

To Thy holy dwelling place
  Thou Thy people safe wilt bring.
They rejoicing in Thy grace,
  Thou enthroned, eternal King.
Well their anthem then may be,
"He hath triumphed gloriously."

# Creation and the Cross

R OLLING wave and dashing spray,
    Cedar tall and daisy bright;
Every sunbeam of the day,
    Every star that gems the night;
All the life of dell and plain;
    Every burst of woodland song;
All combine to swell the strain —
    "God is wise, and God is strong."

Every tear my Saviour shed;
    Traitor's kiss and smiting sore;
Every thorn that pierced His head;
    Yon sad Cross He meekly bore;
Pain and thirst, and darkness drear;
    Grief all other griefs above;
Drooping head and thrusting spear:
    O they tell me, "God is Love."

Bowing low would I adore
    God, the Lord of earth and sea.
Lowlier still, my worship pour,
    When I think of Calvary.
Not creation's glories high,
    So could move my soul within.
Power could spread the spangled sky,
    Love alone my heart could win.

# The Giver

ALL that we have, or great or small,
We owe it, Lord, to Thee.
Thine are the treasures of the earth,
The fulness of the sea.

We plough, we sow, with trembling hope;
God gives the increase still.
We cast the net; but Thou alone
The tide-borne mesh can'st fill.

Blest then be Thou, most bounteous One,
And whilst of Thee we live,
Teach us, so freely thus enriched,
As freely, Lord, to give.

# My Friend

*He careth for you. — 1 Peter 5. 7*

EVERYWHERE, always, close by my side,
Faithful, unchangeable, Christ will abide;
Through sunshine and shadow, through good and through ill,
Seeing me, knowing me, loving me still.

# "I Know"

John 9. 25          2 Cor. 5. 1

1 John 5. 13          Job 19. 25

I do not know how from the sun
  Comes streaming down the glowing ray;
Nor how the responsive pupils sense
  The night, the twilight, and the day.
I do not know what paints the flower;
  Or shades the heath, or tints the sea.
One thing I know, and 'tis enough,
  I once was blind but now I see.

I cannot span the heavens above
  Nor trace the planets' circuit wide;
I cannot give the stars their names
  Nor say which move or which abide.
I cannot tell what lies beyond
  The farthest orb that eye can see;
But this I know — a house in Heaven,
  Not made with hands, God has for me.

I do not know how life begins,
  How flesh and bones take shape and grow;
Nor how the heart to every vein
  Unceasing sends its pulsing flow.
I do not know why breath is breathed,
  Nor how the daily meals sustain:
But God has writ that I may know
  To eternal life I'm born again.

I do not know what lies ahead;
  I cannot see beyond today,
Nor say how soon disease and death
  May waste me to a corpse of clay.
But though the worm my flesh destroy,
  And feed on what is dust in me,
I know that my Redeemer lives,
  And I myself Himself shall see!

# Gethsemane

OVER the brook in the fading light,
Only the privileged three,
Seek with the Lord in the dark'ning night
Gethsemane.

Stone's-cast away on the ground He kneels:
Never an eye wakes to see:
Never a human heart that feels
Christ's agony.

Forged are the nails and the thongs prepared
The beams now are sawn from the tree —
"O Father, this cup — let it yet be spared
If so may be!"

Demons astir, 'tis the time of their power
Oh how dread is their fierce cruelty,
"— But I came to the world for this cause, for this hour,
Let Thy will be!"

Sin of the world, and the damning curse:
God's judgement roars in like the sea:
And the cry is wrung from the olive press
More fervently.

Anguish and crying and tears and blood
Woe's darkest and deep mystery.
And, O can it be, blest Son of God,
'Twas all for me?

Saviour, my soul was a prize so small
Yet what did'st Thou not bear for me!
Take soul and spirit and body, for all
Belongs to Thee!

# Christic and the Waves

Psalm 69          Jonah 2

Matt. 14. 25          Matt. 14. 29

NO standing could my Saviour find
    Deep in the sinking mire;
No refuge from the frowning wave
Of God's consuming ire.
The waters compassed Him about,
    The depths upon Him roll.
The billows spent their tempest force
Upon His sinless soul.

I see Him now, a risen Christ,
    With all his foes and mine
For ever quelled and trodden down
    Beneath His feet divine.
Supreme o'er every adverse wind
    He walks upon the sea,
Looks to my fearful, toiling soul,
    And says, "Come unto Me:

"Come, enter thou by faith upon
    The triumph I have won.
Thy feet may stand where Mine have stood,
    May walk where I have gone.
If I have conquered Death and Hell,
    Where is their vict'ry now?
If I have overcome the world,
    As I am so art thou."

# The Penitent's Prayer

*If Thy presence go not with me, carry us not up hence.*
— Exodus 33. 15

O God, my Father, to Thy throne
    In conscious need I come today;
My sin and failure to bemoan,
    Thy pardon and Thy power to pray.
No help, no hope elsewhere I see;
O let Thy presence go with me!

For too long I've tried to walk alone
    To please myself, to choose my way;
Thy face unsought, Thy will unknown,
    I've wandered farther day by day;
And further still shall err, I know,
Unless Thy presence with me go.

What though the wealth of worlds were mine,
    And carnal pleasures strewed my path;
Could human favour balance Thine,
    Or earthly glory stay Thy wrath?
All, all were vain, an empty show,
Except Thy presence with me go.

O God of Love, of Life, of Light
    To Thee I lift my longing eyes:
O grant me favour in Thy sight,
    My contrite heart do not despise.
Renew the ancient pledge to me,
"I will be with thee certainly."

# The First Day of the Week

*(Tune: 'Kept, safely kept')*

R EMEMBERING Thee!
How blessed so to be:
With every alien though aside
The mind and memory occupied
Alone with Thee.

Whilst thus we meet
In holy, calm retreat
Not only see we Wine and Bread —
Our risen Lord, our living Head,
With Thee we meet.

Yes, Thou art here.
We know, we feel Thee near.
As surely as of old Thou didst
Appear, peace-speaking, in the midst,
The Lord is here!

Thy hands, Thy side,
O Christ, the Crucified,
Once more let us in spirit view,
And draw our melted hearts anew,
Close to Thy side.

There would we rest;
Yea, even on Thy breast:
To prove the sweetness of Thy grace
The heart-beats of Thy love to trace —
Supremely blest!

# A Meditation on Psalm 23

I never shall want: for the Lord is my Shepherd,
    And who ever lacked that was under His care?
He makes me lie down in the fairest of pastures,
    Where soft flow the waters, He leadeth me there.

At times, by the way, I am listless and weary;
    How gently He then doth my spirit restore!
And oft brings me back, when afar I have wandered,
    To walk in the paths of the righteous once more.

Yea, though I should pass through the Valley of Shadows,
    I'll not be afraid: Thou art there by my side.
Thy rod to correct and Thy staff to support me
    Shall still be my comfort, whatever betide.

Though dangers beset and though foes may surround me,
    My table Thou spreadest in face of them still.
With the oil of Thy gladness my head Thou anointest,
    And brimful with blessings my cup dost Thou fill.

O surely Thy goodness, Thy mercy, shall follow
    Attending my footsteps with grace all my days,
Till folded secure in the House of Jehovah
    I'll evermore utter my good Shepherd's praise!

# For Me

WHEN all, like sheep, had gone astray,
And sinned against the light of day,
That Justice might with Love agree,
The Friend of Sinners died for me.

Rejected, scourged, and spit upon,
Betrayed, forsaken, left alone
Accursed of God upon the Tree
The Man of Sorrows died for me.

Nor can the robes of glory hide
The wounds in hands and feet and side.
The scars are there that all may see
The Lord of Glory died for me.

If, ere my day of conflict close,
I must combat the last of foes,
Triumphant still my soul shall be,
The Prince of Life has died for me.


# The Blind Man

*He took the blind man by the hand and led him out of the town. — Mark 8. 23*

LEAD me, my Saviour; take me by the hand,
For Thou can'st see those steps unseen by me.
I cannot walk by sight; 'tis well that Thou hast planned
How I may walk secure by faith in Thee.

Lead me, my Master; let me feel Thy hand,
E'en while Thy face as yet I cannot see.
What though "without the city" I must take my stand,
No-one is lonely while in touch with Thee.

Lead me, Lord Jesus, till at last Thy hand
From my dark blindness sets me gladly free.
The way Thou leadest now I then shall understand,
And, best and brightest, then I'll gaze on Thee.

# Calling and Following

*He arose and followed Jesus. — Matt. 9. 9*

*Jesus arose and followed him. — Matt. 9. 19*

MID the throng and din of cities,
    By the rustic Galilee:
To the bustling man of business
    To the toiler of the sea;
Hark! I hear the Saviour calling,
    Daily calling, "Follow Me."

Is it nothing, all ye people,
    That He thus is drawing near;
Calling still in tones so tender,
    Tones so tender, yet so clear;
Ceaselessly inviting, pleading?
    Who hath ears, O let him hear!

Let him hear, and that sweet summons
    Gladly let him now obey;
Rising quickly, haste to follow
    Closely, humbly, all the way;
Learning more of Christ the Master
    Hour by hour and day by day.

At the silent hour of midnight;
    In the sunshine bright and fair;
In the days of mirth and gladness;
    In the darkest hours of care;
See the Saviour ever listening,
    Listening for His children's prayer.

O, His ear is never heavy,
    And His heart is never cold,
He will catch the sigh, the whisper,
    Read the story they unfold;
And will haste to bring the blessing,
    Ere the tale has half been told.

Yes, 'tis true; but who shall fathom
This amazing mystery;
That the very Lord who called me
Should my patient Listener be;
And the One I fain would follow,
Condescends to "follow" me!

# Even Now

*I know that he shall rise again on the Last Day.*
— John 11. 24

*I know that, even now, whatsoever Thou wilt ask of God,
God will give it Thee.* — John 11. 22

I know, O Lord, a Day shall dawn
Of cloudless glory, endless joy.
When sickness, sighing, tears, nor pain,
Nor death itself, shall come again
To hurt and to destroy.

Then all shall know that all Thy ways
Were ways of mercy, kind and wise.
The mourning eyes shall then be dried,
The longing soul be satisfied,
And those who sleep shall rise.

These things I know: but not alone
For that Last Day my trust shall be.
That very same Almighty power
Dwells in Thee at this present hour,
And those who "trust shall see".

I know it! Whatsoe'er Thou say'st
Thy Father will not disallow,
And though Thou should'st be slow to speak,
Though days are dark, and faith is weak,
I'll trust Thee "even now."

# Through the Waters

Rom. 6. 3-5        Col. 3. 1

INTO death's dark waters faring,
   Christ passed for me;
Shame, reproach and sorrow bearing,
   All, all for me.
Now I spurn the sins that slew Him,
Turn from scenes that never knew Him;
Take my cross and hasten to Him;
   He died for me!

See, the grave has closed around Him,
   Silent and lone;
They who wove the thorns that crowned Him,
   Sealing the stone.
To His tomb have I descended,
Seen my earthly pathway ended;
Here by faith have comprehended
   His grave my own.

O the joy, the blest awaking,
   When Christ arose!
Every band forever breaking,
   My Lord arose.
Free with Him, what tie can bind me?
Safe in Him, what foe can find me?
Death and darkness all behind me,
   With Him I rose.

Sharing in His triumph glorious
   O'er every foe,
Now to walk in life victorious,
   Forward I go.
Where in Heaven, His work completed,
Christ at God's right hand is seated,
There my portion, too, is meted,
   There, there I go.

# The Song Unique

*No man could learn that song but the Hundred and forty and four thousand.* — Rev. 14. 3

A MID the blended harmony that fills
   The Courts of Glory, hark, a new note thrills,
So strangely sweet, so sweetly strange, that they
Whose song it is, alone can learn the lay.

For they had toiled where others had not shared.
They had endured what none but they had dared.
Weeping, they learned yon song that fills the skies;
None, e'en in Heaven, can learn it otherwise.

O heart bereft! were trials ne'er like thine?
None, then, has learned, as thou, the Heart Divine.
From griefs unique, and lonely struggles striven,
Have come the songs unmatched — in earth and Heaven.

# "I Will Sing"

1 Cor. 14. 15

H OW *can* I stop singing, so wondrously blest?
   The sins that defiled me, the cares that distressed,
Are all swept away, and my soul is set free;
I cannot but praise Him, He's so good to me.

He's the Star of my midnight, the Sun of my day,
The Bread of my table, the Strength of my way;
My Joy beyond telling, my measureless Peace;
I must, I will praise Him — O how can I cease!

Though fig-tree and vineyard no substance should yield,
Though the stall should be empty, and barren the field;
Yea, all through the Valley, my praise shall ascend
To Him, my Redeemer, my Shepherd, my Friend.

Then, life and its trials all over and done,
The warfare accomplished, the victory won;
No jar in the music, no sob in the song,
I'll praise Him and bless Him, eternity long!

# Fruit, Blossom and Bud

*The rod of Aaron . . . budded, and brought forth buds,*
*and bloomed blossoms, and yielded almonds. — Num. 17. 8*

I FEAST on the fruit that He bears
  And O it is sweet to my taste;
The virtues and glories He wears,
  The beauties wherewith He is graced.

But still as I study Him more,
  And ponder His words and his ways,
New beauties unnoticed before
  Are blossoming out to my gaze.

And humbly, yet gladly, I own,
  Though daily new glimpses I get,
There's many a glory unknown
  That's still in the bud to me yet.

Yes, such is His fulness, and such
  The freshness and dew of His youth,
Time's withering hand cannot touch
  His treasures of goodness and truth.

He's the Rod and the Branch and the Root,
  And still to my wondering soul,
Will bud and will bloom and bear fruit
  While years of Eternity roll.

# Communion

Song of Sol. 2. 10-17

M Y Beloved spake to me, and so winning was His tone:
'O arise, my love, my fair one, come away!
For the winter-time is past; lo, the rains are over-blown,
And the sward with new-bloomed flowerets all is gay.
Hark, the turtle's voice is cooing
Gentle love-notes, softly wooing;
All the air's athrill with gladsome song to-day.
Here the fig-tree yields its flavour,
There the vine gives forth its savour.
O arise, my love, my fair one, come away!

'O my dove that dwellest safe, with the Clefted Rock thy seat,
Thou that shelterest in the Secret of the Stair;
Let me hear thy voice, my love, for thy voice indeed is sweet,
Turn thy countenance to me, divinely fair.
Ah, but let us, quickly hasting,
Seize the little foxes wasting
All the tenderest grapes that grace our vineyard rare.
For, alas, what fruits are sweetest
They would rob and spoil the fleetest;
O then guard thy vintage well, thou only-fair!'

Then with heart all welling o'er, to my Love I answered low:
My Beloved, I am His and He is mine,
Where He tends and feeds His flock 'mong the lilies I will go,
Where He makes them rest at noon will I recline.
Till the soft day-dawn awaking,
Through the flying shadows breaking,
Brings the One I love to me, for Him I'll pine.
O that like the young hart bounding,
Thou would'st skip those hills surrounding,
That they never more might sever Thee and Thine!

# The Bowed Head

John 19. 30

M EEKLY He bows His sacred head to die.
The agony, the shame, are almost o'er,
The parchèd lips have framed their last lone cry.
The tender heart of Christ can bear no more.
But yet He bows the head, submissive still,
E'en at the hour of death, to all the Father's will.

Be still, proud heart! How can I stand and gaze
Upon that Head, so meekly bending low,
And not lament, with tears and shame of face,
Thy wilful ways, rebelling, murmuring so?
O for the grace, in every earthly loss,
To bow the head to God. So Christ did on the Cross.


# The Prayer of Moses

*I beseech Thee, show me Thy glory.* — Exod. 33. 18

A S prayed Thy favoured saint of old
We cry, 'Thy glory, Lord, unfold.'
Pass Thou before our raptured eyes,
Great, Holy, Gracious, Faithful, Wise.

No longer with averted face
Hide'st Thou the radiance of Thy grace:
Thy Son has come, in Him we see,
Unveiled, the Face of Deity.

Yet dim our sight, our spirits slow
To learn of Him we fain would know.
So still we plead, as he of old,
'Thy glory, O our God, unfold!'

# Altogether Lovely

*This is my Beloved, and this is my Friend.*
— Song of Sol. 5. 16

C HILD of the lowly Maid,
    Born in the stable mean;
Plying the workman's trade,
    Jesus the Nazarene:
Buried in Jordan's stream,
    Fasting in desert bare;
Hail Him, the Lord supreme!
    Hail Him, the only-Fair!

Healing the halt and blind,
    Touching at the leper's sore;
Soothing the anxious mind;
    Weeping at death's dark door:
Teaching with timely word,
    Tending with patient care;
Hail Him, the glorious Lord!
    Hail Him, the only-Fair!

Bowing in anguish down,
    Praying with cries and tears;
Wearing the thorny crown,
    Hearing the cruel jeers;
Dying as none could die,
    Bearing what none could bear:
Hail Him, the Lord Most High!
    Hail Him, the only-Fair!

Bursting the bands of death,
    Rending the vanquished grave,
Breathing the Spirit's breath,
    Mighty to help and save:
Reigning in glory bright;
    Coming in grandeur rare:
Hail Him, my heart's delight,
    Ever the only-Fair!

# Hallelujah!

Psa. 148

**H**ALLELUJAH! Hallelujah! Let the heavens declare His name;
Let the heights of highest glory all His majesty proclaim.
Let His angels all adore Him;
Ye, His hosts, fall down before Him.
Hallelujah! Hallelujah! Praise His name!

Sun and moon, repeat the story! Tell His praise, ye stars of light!
Let the splendour of the Heavens evermore extol His might.
He hath stablished them for ever;
His decree it faileth never.
Hallelujah! Hallelujah! Praise His name!

Let the earth and teeming ocean join their voice the strain to swell.
Let the elements that serve Him His supremacy forth tell.
Lofty peaks of rugged feature;
Fruitful fields: yea, every creature:
Hallelujah! Hallelujah! Praise His name!

Kings and peoples, bend before Him! Rulers, hail the only Lord!
Young and old, the youth, the maiden, to His name the praise accord.
Name sublime! Alone excelling
All in earth or Heaven dwelling.
Hallelujah! Hallelujah! Praise His name!

Mighty chorus, mingling, blending, hear its cadence rise and fall!
Ye, His saints, can ye be silent, ye who owe Him most of all?
Ye, of all His creatures nighest,
Well may raise your notes the highest.
Hallelujah! Hallelujah! Praise His name!

# The Great Sight

*Then were the disciples glad when they saw the Lord.*
— John 20. 20

O UR hearts are glad, for we have seen the Lord;
   The living Lord, victorious o'er the grave.
O joy to see Him, joy to hear His word,
   Our Lord and Master, strong to bless and save!

His hands, His feet, He showed us, and the place
   Where deeply pierced at last the cruel spear.
O precious scars! O deathless love and grace
   That still in those redeeming wounds appear!

Most wondrous sight! All else is poor and dim
   To eyes that thus have viewed the Risen One.
All power is His, all glories meet in Him,
   The sinner's Saviour, God's beloved Son.

So we are glad, our spirits all aglow,
   Filled with a new and strangely thrilling joy.
Power from Himself inbreathing, forth we go;
   O may His service all our days employ.

# The Burden-Bearer

I KNOW the Son of God for me
  The Cross endured.
I know He suffered in my stead,
And, by the precious blood He shed,
  My peace secured.

I know the Man who died for me
  Is on the Throne.
I know He ever watches there,
With sympathising shepherd-care,
  O'er all His own.

So why should I not trust His love
  And power Divine?
If He could bear my sins away,
Can He not carry day by day
  Those cares of mine?

My burdens, then, my frets, my fears,
  On Him I'll cast.
I'll leave my life in His good hand,
Assured my path in love He's planned
  From first to last.

Thus gladly on my homeward way
  I'll singing go;
Until, by His abounding grace,
At last I see Him face to face
  Who loved me so.